The C

Other titles in Heroes of the Cross *series*

Brother Andrew
Gladys Aylward
William Booth
Catherine Bramwell–Booth
Amy Carmichael
Corrie
Jim Elliott
Elizabeth Fry
Wilfred Grenfell
Helen Keller
C. S. Lewis
Eric Liddell
David Livingstone
Martin Luther
Martin Luther King
George Müller
Jackie Pullinger
Christina Rossetti
Mary Slessor
John and Betty Stam
C. T. Studd
Hudson Taylor
George Thomas, Lord Tonypandy
John Welch
John Wesley
Richard Wurmbrand

The Cambridge Seven

For Christ and China

Joan Clifford

MARSHALL PICKERING

First published in Great Britain in 1990 by Marshall Pickering

Marshall Pickering is an imprint of
Collins Religious Division
part of the Collins Publishing Group
8 Grafton Street, London W1X 3LA

Text Set in Palatino by Selectmove Ltd
Printed in Great Britain by
Cox and Wyman Ltd, Reading, Berks.

Dedication

For Sylvia Fulton

Contents

Acknowledgements

The author wishes to express appreciation of the assistance given by the following: Miss Anne Edwards and the Overseas Missionary Fellowship, Miss Elizabeth Williams and the Partnership House Library, Dr Oliver Barclay and Mrs Edith Staines.

Joan Clifford

The following books were particularly helpful:

The Cambridge Seven, John Pollock (Marshalls 1985).
C.T. Studd and Priscilla, Eileen Vincent (Kingsway 1988).
C.T. Studd, Kathleen White (Marshalls 1985).
James Hudson Taylor, Howard Taylor (Hodder 1973).
A Missionary Band (Broomhall 1886).
First Years in China (Williams 1886).
Hudson Taylor & China's Open Century, Book VI, Broomhall (Hodder 1988).

Chapter 1

Seven reach China

It was the 18th March, 1885. The harbour of the great Chinese port of Shanghai was alive with craft – a vast quantity of gaily painted junks, sampans, grain ships and steam tenders which had made their way from the mouth of the mighty Yangtze up the lesser river Wang-po. Waiting on the landing-stage was a slightly- built man of middle years, not a very significant-looking person. Clad in full Chinese dress, only a close inspection would reveal him to be a European. His name was Hudson Taylor and he was the Director of the China Inland Mission.

Hudson was perhaps thinking of the first time that he himself, twenty years before, had landed on this shore. He had then been friendless and totally unsupported – except by the hand of God. He remembered the deep loneliness he had felt at first with not a friend or acquaintance anywhere near – no single hand to welcome him or anyone who even knew his name. He also remembered the tears of thankfulness that he had then shed because he had at last come to the land of his destiny.

His expression now changed to one of eagerness. Disembarking from the steam tender was a chattering company of seven young men, each in his early twenties. They were the focus of all eyes. Well-built, handsome, confident-looking, they wore good European suits and smiling faces, and one sensed a great camaraderie among them. Their fair-skinned English countenances contrasted markedly with the appearance of the dark-haired, darker-skinned Chinese around them. The seven could not be overlooked.

The young men looked about them, unsure. Hudson Taylor hurried forward to greet them with a fervent 'Welcome! Welcome!' They were bound to suffer 'culture shock' but they were not arriving friendless or unexpected. They had come by arrangement to join Hudson and to serve the mission.

They were carried in open chairs down winding streets and over crossings and bridges through the great walled city, a vast commercial centre. They were taken to the foreign settlement, where lived consuls, merchants and missionaries; some, like the commercial bosses or 'taipans', in luxury, some more modestly, and some, like those at the China Inland Mission, in stark simplicity. A stone's-throw from the British Consulate, Hudson had rented two houses in the Yuan Ming Yuan building, one for offices and one as a temporary home for the new arrivals. The premises were extremely bare but the seven were not expecting luxury; they had come to serve.

It was all strange. At night, after more welcomes and a meal, they attempted to sleep, not easy with so much going round in their minds. One of the seven, Stanley Smith, recorded the day's events in his diary. He scribbled – 'We have arrived in Shanghai March 18th. It was very solemn, landing on the shores of this vast empire and feeling the need in a deepening sense . . . but His gracious promises cover our fears . . . .'

Willie Cassels wrote to his family. 'It was with full hearts that we set foot for the first time on the soil of this dear country to which the Lord has called us. What was our first thought as we went through these streets and gazed on the numbers of Chinese that met us at every turn? It was an almost overwhelming thought of the enormous work that waits to be done . . . we felt more than ever that nothing but a mighty outpouring of the spirit of God can be of any use . . . .'

The China to which the seven came was full of tension and uncertainty. The great Empire of the Manchus was said to be 'rotten at its heart and breaking up at its extremities'. Under the intrigues of the Empress Ci Xi, who knew what might not happen? But the China Inland Mission, firmly set on evangelising the whole of mighty China for Jesus Christ, had

150 staff members and was on a crest, all set for expansion. And now it was joined by seven remarkable young men who would add a formidable strength to the progress of the mission. They were already known in England as the 'Cambridge Seven'. That night Hudson Taylor entered their names in his ledger – Montague Beauchamp, William Cassels, Dixon Hoste, brothers Arthur and Cecil Polhill-Turner, Stanley Smith and Charles Studd. They were known to one another as: Monty, Willie, Dick, Arthur, Cecil, Stanley and Charley. They were now ready for their assault on the evil forces of superstition and ignorance to be encountered in this amazing empire.

Chapter 2

How it all began

Back in the United Kingdom, the 'Cambridge Seven' were quite famous especially among Christian people who followed their activities with pride. But a far wider circle of people, who had no connection with the institutional church, could not help noticing the impact already made by these young men; their names seemed to be always in the news.

In those Victorian days it was not a common event for five rich, well-connected, talented young graduates and two young professional Army officers to offer their services to a missionary society and make it clear that they were willingly giving up the prospects of lives of luxury and influence for an unknown future. But that is what had taken place. Not only that, but the missionary society to which they were now contracted was considered by many as rather an eccentric one; it had extraordinary rules, such as the requirement to wear Chinese dress and to depend entirely upon God for the day-to-day running of one's life.

Moreover, the China Inland Mission (CIM) had no responsibility to any particular church body, but accepted Christian workers from all branches of the Church or none, provided they agreed upon the central tenets of the Christian Faith. The principles laid down by Hudson Taylor as the mission evolved were strictly held, and were regarded strangely by other and more traditional missionary societies. Their lifestyle was thought to be definitely 'eccentric'. And the determination of the mission to encompass the entire huge Chinese Empire for its evangelistic field caused some raised eyebrows.

None of this criticism bothered Hudson Taylor, who saw his methods working well. All his principles and ideas had been thoroughly explained to the young men of Cambridge before they embarked on their offering of themselves. And they felt honoured to have been accepted as members of the mission.

The group was known as the 'Cambridge Seven' because they had all met either at the University or through relatives and friends at the University. Some had been friends since their boyhood at their public schools. Monty, Stanley and Willie had all been educated at Repton, and Charley, Arthur and Cecil at Eton. And along with Dick, who had been at Clifton College, they were quite likely to meet in London Society. For all the young men came from comfortable, even luxurious homes in London and the counties. In the ordered Victorian system of the time, with 'the rich man in his castle and the poor man at his gate', the Cambridge Seven came from an enviable stratum of society. They had all known delightful, spacious childhoods, happy family life and had every opportunity for pleasure and personal development. They had no problems about receiving further education or worries about 'good jobs' at the end of it. Everything was laid on for them to ensure glittering futures. And since they knew nothing with which to compare this lifestyle, they did not realise that it was anything unusual or privileged.

It also so happened that the seven came from homes where the Christian religion was honoured, if only in a traditional church-going manner. Some of the parents took their faith very seriously and it was passed on to their sons. Stanley Smith's father, a successful surgeon, was unashamedly Christian: the home of Monty Beauchamp was a noted centre of evangelical activity: Willie Cassels came from a godly home and, according to his brother, had decided as early as thirteen that he would take Holy Orders and become a clergyman. General and Mrs Hoste, Dick's parents, followed a formal, garrison-type religion but were committed Christians of a somewhat strict kind.

Charley Studd had seen very clearly the effect of religion upon his father although at an early age he had not always appreciated it. Edward Studd, a rich, retired jute planter, returned from India, had been soundly converted by the ministry of the dramatic American evangelists Moody and Sankey. As a result, he had sold his racehorses, given up many pleasure-seeking activities and caused his coachman to say, 'There's the same skin but there's a new man inside'.

To tell the truth, Edward's new mode of life was a constant challenge to his family. Charley said of his father: 'Everyone in the house led a dog's life till they were converted . . . in the day I crept round the other side of the house when I saw him coming!' However, the Studd parents continued to give their boys and girls a luxurious life at their Wiltshire home, Tedworth.

All the young men came from large Victorian families and never lacked for company. They had all that growing young people could desire. They were all keen on sport and were offered all the necessary facilities. Cricket pitches were laid out on the Studd estate; in the winter they skated on the frozen Serpentine lake in London. They could ride and hunt on fine horses, row on the rivers, swim, play tennis on their own marked-out courts, cycle on the latest amazing bicycles. They relished this freedom and rather took it for granted. They knew no different. In their homes they were waited on by retinues of servants.

Yet Christian influences were always coming to bear upon them. The Repton boys had been persuaded, in their schooldays, to go to a small prayer group set up by the Honourable Granville Waldegrave, Monty's cousin. This was held in a room over the Repton tuck-shop and became quite famous.

When they went up to Cambridge, their Christian commitment was constantly challenged, and, although they did not realise it, Christ was calling them to His service and would not let them go.

The universities at this time were not particularly 'religious' places and it required courage and determination to attempt greater witness than sporadic attendance at the college chapels. There was a certain amount of academic work to be completed, though many of the wealthy lads (no girls then) would not need a degree to help them on their way in life. If an undergraduate was an eldest son, and expected to inherit, he knew that his task would be to live a gentlemanly existence running the family estate and doing a great deal of travelling; the second son would probably go into a good regiment as was the case with Cecil Polhill-Turner. A third son in the family often went 'into the Church' and lived a life of respectable conventional churchmanship in a family living.

There were, as always, genuine academics but there was no need for the Cambridge Seven to struggle competitively to gain a Ph.D.

As well as work, there were the delights of

university life. There was pride in being 'up' at one of England's two oldest universities and being members of the gracious old colleges. Four of the seven were at Trinity with its grassy quadrangle, its fountain, and its marvellous library. This was supposedly founded by Henry VIII in 1546. One of the seven was at St John's, and one had been up at Jesus. In spring and summer they all relished the beautiful lawns and tree-lined banks known as 'The Backs', which stretch along the course of the River Cam, a lovely sight to enjoy or to show to relatives and girl-friends. University life could be a heady existence.

There were excellent opportunities for sports and athletics and in these the Cambridge band revelled.

Stanley, though hampered by serious illness at the end of his school life and always the prey of chest troubles, was madly keen on rowing. His extra skills here were quickly noted and led ultimately to his becoming stroke of the 'varsity boat and gaining his 'blue' – the coveted badge awarded to supreme university athletes.

Monty was also a fine oarsman and rowed regularly for the First Trinity Eight. Willie enjoyed rowing, too, in a more modest way, and had missed his soccer blue only because of a broken leg. Both the Polhill-Turner brothers were sporty, keen on football and particularly on cricket. Arthur received his colours in 1879 from the hands of Charley Studd.

Charley would probably remain as the most enduring name of the seven, the one of the group then known to every Englishman during the next year or two. For he became one of the most famous cricketers of his day. Years of playing on his father's private pitch led to brilliant results in going up to Trinity and he won his blue and played for Cambridge for four consecutive years. He came from a family mad on cricket. The great W.G. Grace, the most famous of all cricketers of the Victorian age, described Charley Studd as 'the most brilliant member of a well-known cricketing family. His batting and bowling was very good . . . his style of batting was free and correct and he scored largely and rapidly against the best bowlers of his time.'

Studd became a household name. In 1882 he played in Australia with the MCC in the team which recovered the 'Ashes'. He found a great thrill in the game and it absorbed much of his time and thought – what could ever prove more exciting?

Two other future members of the seven were not up at Cambridge but were soon to be deeply involved in Christian activities there through friends and relatives. These were Dixon (Dick) Hoste, a gunner subaltern from a military family and brother of William Hoste of Trinity, and Cecil Polhill-Turner who had obtained a commision in a stylish regiment, the 2nd Dragoon Guards. He was brother to Arthur Polhill-Turner of Trinity. Both these men enjoyed the social and athletic life of their regiments.

With so much sport and lively social life, the Christian commitment of the Cambridge friends tended to become sporadic. Prayer groups were attended when remembered; 'quiet times' not always taken; the newly-formed Christian Union not always supported; religion did not always seem very real or important. Yet two interlocking strands of concern led the young men nearer to decision-time.

One strand was the powerful influence upon the universities of the American evangelists Moody and Sankey. The other strand was the influence of the seven and their families upon each other. There were also the casual, if providential, meetings with people who made the undergraduates think, and challenged them afresh to a deeper Christian commitment. Stanley, taking up a holiday tutorship in Lowestoft, was introduced to a Mr Price, an elderly Christian, an ordinary enough person, but one with whom he could talk freely about spiritual things. Mr Price showed Stanley that there was quite a bit of selfishness in him that an easygoing life had not yet checked.

When it was announced that a Moody and Sankey mission would be held in Cambridge, there was some amusement. It was not to be taken seriously. But all undergraduates received a personal invitation signed by Charley's eldest brother, Kynaston, who was already a committed Christian. Some of the colleges laughed at the idea of two rather uneducated, rough Americans coming to their seats of learning to preach to them. Even Kynaston was a bit worried about their reception.

When the time came for the first meeting, on Guy Fawkes night 1882, many undergraduates went along just to make themselves a nuisance and, in their words, 'have a bit of fun'. There was much rowdiness before the meeting began and some Trinity men piled up chairs into a pyramid and things rapidly got out of control. It was not a very conducive setting for a successful mission.

Arthur had gone along and felt that their behaviour was not very sporting. He was quite impressed with the address by Moody, a vigorous preacher with a broad American accent. Sankey sang and some listened. Afterwards, many men were rather ashamed of themselves. But almost immediately there were tales of huge crowds hurrying to the subsequent meetings; of the most unlikely people seeking counsel and making declarations for Christ; of men mounting the iron ladder to the enquiry room, where quiet personal talks took place and new beginnings were sealed. Arthur attended a further meeting. This time he was strangely moved by Moody and felt in him 'a true tinge of manliness'. 'His searching address began to penetrate.' Moody talked of the Prodigal Son and of the hollow, drifting life followed by so many of the audience. This time there were no interruptions – his hearers knew that he was right. On the final day of the mission, at a packed gathering in the Corn Exchange, Moody spoke out very directly: 'Will those who have received blessing during the week please stand as a token of their faith?' Over 200 people rose; Arthur Polhill-Turner was one of them.

The Moody mission had both awakened people for the first time and also revived those whose faith had burnt low. One of these was Willie Hoste of Trinity. Quite renewed, he was full of enthusiasm when he went to visit his parents in Brighton and found his young brother Dick there on winter leave. Strangely – or providentially – the Moody mission had now moved to Brighton. Of course Willie was anxious to take his brother along. Mrs Hoste had already invited Dick to go with her and the General but, courteously, Dick had declined and sat reading his newspaper at the time when they would be leaving for the inaugural meeting. Willie, who had just arrived, ran in and hurried up to his young brother. 'Come on, Dick', he said urgently, 'put on your coat and come with me to the meeting.' Almost before he knew what he was doing, Dick had done so and found himself under the spell of the charismatic Moody.

He found himself surprisingly attracted by this ordinary, rather rough-looking layman and even more by the prayers uttered by the man. He had never before heard anyone speak so simply to God, as though to a friend. And the address given by Moody also stirred him deeply. He felt dissatisfied with his present life, despite his love of the Army. Now began a time of inner struggle for Dick, who had planned for himself a traditional military career, as was the custom in his family. He was an ambitious soldier. But he began to ask himself, 'What does God really want with my life?' By the end of the Brighton mission the struggle was resolved. Dick had offered his heart totally to Christ. General and Mrs Hoste, along with William, had the thrill of seeing their younger son walk up the aisle of the Dome Mission Hall in open confession of his Christian faith.

In their different ways, the Cambridge Seven found Christ in a new and personal sense. Monty Beauchamp, from a particularly effective Christian background, had yet remained a fairly formal believer for several years. But when up at Trinity, he had been the subject of prayers by his friends Stanley Smith and Kynaston Studd. These prayers availed and before long Monty was writing to tell them that he had 'yielded all to Christ'.

Later in his life, Charley Studd made very

plain the stages of his spiritual journey. He said: 'I always knew that Christ was the Saviour of the whole world; but, until a certain moment, I had never known He was my Saviour.' Charley was brought to a personal relationship with Christ on the illness of his brother George. 'As night after night I watched by his bedside as he was hovering between life and death, God showed me what the honour, what the pleasure, what the riches of this world were worth. All these things had become as nothing to my brother. He cared only about the Bible and the Lord Jesus Christ and God taught me the same lesson.'

There were inner struggles now for Charley. His passion for cricket had absorbed so much of his time and thinking, but in this new spirit he decided to put God first. He now wanted his team not only to win their games, but also and more, to put their whole lives under Christ. He had a long way to go but he was a different man. In London in 1884 he knew a new peace. He knelt down and said aloud two lines from a hymn by Frances Ridley Havergal –

'Take my life and let it be
consecrated Lord to Thee.'

And he truly meant it.

Chapter 3

The Compulsion

The whirlwind Christian experience stirred up by the Moody and Sankey revival had almost immediate results among the Cambridge band, as they were then known. Under the compulsion of Christ, the members began to turn to various forms of Christian service and to discover their own particular talents. Stanley Smith found that he possessed the gift of oratory; when speaking in public he could hold an audience, whether in a large hall or in the open air. He faced the crowds in Hyde Park beside the Reformers' tree near Marble Arch and found that he could connect with strolling folk of fashion and equally with the roughs who came to jeer and heckle. He was a handsome man of athletic build and great charm. He also began to carry out Christian work in a soldiers' home in Aldershot.

Some of the seven began to work among the poor; this they did seemingly without embarrassment but gradually they began to be aware of social distinctions. Charley Studd wrote to his mother: 'Finding out about the poor has increased my horror at the luxurious way I have been living; so many suits while thousands are starving and perishing of cold, so all must be sold before I come home . . . ' This was the beginning of an ascetic stance adopted increasingly by Charley, who had decided that he could really manage in life with very little.

As the students came to the end of their university life, they had to make decisions about their futures. These, they all realised, would be different now that they had so dramatically and genuinely made over their lives to Christ and His service. Such new life would probably mean renouncing the comfortable futures they would have known. It might well mean arguments with families and friends and perhaps ostracism, especially for the two soldiers, Dick and Cecil. But they knew they must face this. Actually deciding what to do was the biggest problem.

Willie Cassels, not a man of worrying spiritual crises, took Holy Orders and went as a curate to a large London parish in Kennington. Here at All Saints in south London, he threw himself into the work. There were the huge Sunday schools of the day and 'hard work among thousands of railway men connected with the Nine Elms works of the London and S.W. railway.' Willie was a quiet person, in fact among his Cambridge friends he had been known as 'William the Silent', but when he did speak, he spoke sense. He was a neat, fastidious man but quite able to dominate any crowd in his own quiet way.

Arthur Polhill-Turner was expected to take up the family clerical living and began to read for ordination at Ridley Hall. But he had been deeply stirred by events and was not sure that this was going to be enough for him.

Charley Studd was very unsure about his future. At one point he decided to read for the Bar, but was still not certain.

After taking his degree and with the excitement of the Henley Regatta behind him, Stanley Smith went to teach in a preparatory school owned by his brother-in-law. But he was always going off to meetings and talking with his old friends. He too was unclear about the future.

Monty Beauchamp was also vague. From the quiet luxury of his family home, Langley Park in Norfolk, he went up to Ridley Hall and began to read for Holy Orders. Then he too had doubts and left.

The 'soldier athletes' had their own problems. Both Dick Hoste and Cecil Polhill-Turner felt that they were not fulfilling their destinies. It would be for them terribly hard to give up their army careers, in which they were both deeply absorbed, but they were sure there was something else intended for them. General Hoste was against Dick doing anything peremptory;

he bade him wait for a while to be sure that his 'call' was genuine. And Cecil was finding it hard to quit the Guards, where he loved the immaculate drill, the ceremonial occasions and the sporting life.

Then the situation gradually crystallised for all the men. The call to missionary work and to the work in China came. First it was a whisper, then louder, then finally a clamour which could not be stifled. They were all under a total compulsion.

This call probably arose because Hudson Taylor, head of the China Inland Mission, was a friend of the Beauchamp family. Sir Thomas and Lady Beauchamp thoroughly approved of the way in which he was working and had supported him from his early days in China. They had given him hospitality in their lovely home when he was in England, and one of Monty's earliest memories concerned Hudson. As a little boy of five, Monty had been given a set of chopsticks by Hudson and had enjoyed playing about with them, trying to eat in the true Chinese way. He had also played with the *bianzi* or pigtail which Hudson used to wear. The Beauchamps always attended meetings at which Hudson spoke when on furlough, and the relationship was fresh and continuing. So it was natural that this interest should seep into Monty himself and be passed on to his friends. They in their turn could not but be impressed by the record of Hudson's achievements.

Hudson was no born orator but somehow his words always remained with people and caused them to examine their own lives and to be moved to support him. And his life confirmed his words.

So it was natural that Monty should talk to his chum Stanley Smith about China. Finally, Stanley received what he considered absolute guidance. When turning to his Bible, he read: 'I will also give thee for a light to the gentiles, that thou mayest be my salvation unto the ends of the earth.' This was it – he must go to China!

Stanley now persuaded his friend Willie Cassels. In his diary he wrote: 'I went down to see Cassels in Lambeth. Had a nice talk at lunch . . . . I trust he now sees his way definitely to go to China.' Cassels would have liked to go out under the banner of the Anglican missionary society but they were not then planning to go into the interior of China and this was the thrilling charge that Hudson laid upon his followers.

After his period of uncertainty, Charley Studd knew also that his next step had been decided. 'It was not long before God led me to go to China', he said. He had gone to the farewell meeting of the famous missionary John McCarthy, one of the CIM 'giants', and this was his turning point.

Monty Beauchamp had been busy acting as 'China broker' for his friends but had not himself considered the missionary life. Suddenly he came upon a little booklet called *A strange but true story* about the claims of the mission field. This affected him deeply and was decisive. He made up his mind also to go to China.

Dick Hoste was also coming to the same decision. He had heard much about the CIM from his brother William and was always receiving mission books from him, probably passed on from Monty. Dick said he was 'deeply impressed by the single-hearted, self-denying devotion to the cause of the Gospel in China of Hudson Taylor.' He also admired 'the lines of simple and direct faith in God for temporal supply and protection . . . and the close identification of the missionaries with the Chinese people . . . . '

Miraculously at this time, he heard from his father, General Hoste, that opposition had been withdrawn to Dick resigning his commission, and his father would now wish him 'God speed' in the Chinese venture.

The Polhill-Turner brothers had been holding evangelistic meetings in their mother's drawing-room, though she was not too enthusiastic. They too began to be conscious of a pull towards China, about which so many people they admired were now talking. Surely the 'five' ought to be seven.

The seven now had various hurdles to face. The main one – would Hudson Taylor accept them? In spite of their newfound Christian humility, they could see they might be thought of as 'good catches' for the mission – rich, personable, well-educated and quite influential. But Hudson would not take 'just anyone'. He did not, he said, need any 'loafers'. There were letters and interviews. Hudson quietly put to them the principles of the mission and stressed all the difficulties and possible dangers that might confront them. Could they face these? They must have convinced him because all were accepted.

The excitement of the religious revival among the universities was increased by the announcement of the Cambridge men's future. There was a particular excitement to the general public in the decision of Charley Studd and Stanley Smith. One newspaper spoke of 'the extraordinary interest aroused by the announcement that the captain of the Cambridge eleven and the stroke oar of the Cambridge boat were going out as missionaries.' Both men were considerable public figures, well-known and popular among both the University set and the general public for their athletic successes.

A formidable problem to be overcome was 'the family'. Despite the encouragement to a dedicated Christian life of most of the families, leaving for the remote Far East for an indefinite period was another matter. Several of the men had lost their fathers early in life and the plight of the widowed mothers was understandable. Mrs Cassels was distressed at the thought of 'losing' William. She had been a widow for many years and all the rest of her seven sons were already abroad, probably serving the Victorian Empire somewhere. She went so far as to call on Hudson Taylor and beg him not to take William away from her. It was difficult for Hudson. He and Cassels prayed a lot about this and, in October 1884, a letter from Mrs Cassels recognised that William 'sees it as his duty and privilege to enter upon the Chinese mission work'. She therefore 'could not take the part of a bad mother to one of the best of sons.' She would put no further obstacles in the way. William was sad for her but believed he had to go.

Mrs Studd was even more distraught. She wept and wept; there was deep depression in the home. Again many prayers were said. No son wanted willingly to wound his mother, but Charley was now convinced he had to leave. On a November night, Charley said afterwards, 'I could not go to sleep but it seemed that I heard these words over and over – 'Ask of me and I shall give thee the heathen for thine inheritance and the uttermost parts of the earth for thy possession.' These words from the psalms convinced him of the importance of his call to China. When his mother realised that Charley was settled in his decision and that it was not a passing whim, she withdrew her opposition and supported him gamely for the remainder of her life. It was to cost her a great deal. The social position of the Cambridge men had its own problems. Should they not remain in the life to which they had been born and carry out the duties of their various inheritances? What of their responsibilities to the estates? What of the fortunes they might be expected to inherit and the use of such monies? The men had to face this one. Mrs Polhill-Turner was not happy about her sons going off to work on the Hudson Taylor mission. They were English gentlemen and as such had appropriate duties. Cecil might have to forfeit an inheritance from a bachelor uncle if he went. Cecil and Arthur, though their decisions to go to China were made at the latest hour, were equally determined.

In the end, they agreed to sail 'without being formally connected with the mission'. Thus they would observe the nature of the work before being totally committed. This enabled their mother to speak of her sons as 'travelling in China'. For some reason, she was hard to convince that they were going on a noble enterprise. There seemed little doubt that the two young men would be on the mission roll in due course. Cecil now resigned his commission.

There now began a hectic round of farewell meetings, the length and breadth of the country and in Scotland, too. Everywhere the young Cambridge group was welcomed and their words heard with appreciation. The young men were swept along on a great tide of spiritual vitality.

This was quite amazing. Someone said: 'Students are apt to regard professedly religious men of their own age as wanting in manliness, unfit for the river or the cricket field and only good for psalm singing and pulling long faces!'

But the students were impressed when the big muscular hands and long arms of the ex-captain of the Cambridge eight stretched out in entreaty, while he eloquently told the old, old story of redeeming love.

Matters moved swiftly. The sailing for China was planned for the spring of 1885. Modest luggage was assembled. Three great farewell gatherings were arranged at which the Cambridge Seven would speak – in Oxford, Cambridge and finally in London at the Exeter Hall. All the meetings were crammed but the London gathering outstripped all the others. On the platform sat forty Cambridge undergraduates and above their heads hung a huge map of China, while on the table lay a pile of Chinese New Testaments. As the appropriate hour struck, the Chairman entered followed by the seven young, prospective missionaries. They were obviously men of bearing, education and position. In turn they spoke briefly. Each gave a personal testimony as to what had happened within himself and why he was going to China. Stanley Smith spoke brilliantly, Charley Studd gruffly and sincerely, Arthur Polhill-Turner, the youngest, spoke just a few lines. But the message of them all found its mark. Out of love of their Master they were offering Him their lives, to carry the Gospel to those who knew it not. The rain poured down outside but within the hall the atmosphere was electric. Never had there been a missionary meeting like this. The Cambridge Seven left like young heroes.

There was now little time to go; a few private moments with families, promises of letters and prayers, much hugging and kissing. Willie Cassels had printed in red letters on his luggage the words GOD FIRST. Then the 5th February, 1885, dawned. A great gaggle of relatives and friends were present at Victoria Railway Station. Some people came to scoff – 'We'll give you a year or two at the most, then you'll be back'. Porters muttered – 'They're off their 'eads!' But the seven were greatly cheered by the atmosphere on the station, despite the rumours, later confirmed, of the death of General Gordon in Khartoum. Mothers, sisters, cousins, friends – a great company of wellwishers swept along the platform as the boat train drew in. It was a company full of prayer and encouragement.

The moment came, the whistle blew, it was ten o'clock and the train steamed out. The seven stood with heads out of the windows until the figures on the platform became minute and finally passed out of sight. The seven looked at one another. They were on their way to China.

Chapter 4

Tough Training

On arrival in Shanghai, the seven were plunged into a whirlpool of activity. They felt battered by unfamiliar sounds, sights and smells. No matter how much they had read and heard about China, the actual experience of really being there was overwhelming. They were being introduced to a new way of life and at first, in the foreign settlement, things were comparatively straightforward. Here were many Europeans and English-speakers and meetings in the familiar pattern were quickly arranged for the much-publicised seven to make their witness. There were meetings for cricket club and rowing club athletes at the Royal Asiatic Society and in the Lyceum theatre. In this strangely mixed, excitable place, the Cambridge Seven began their overseas missionary work. Speaking here was not much different from speaking at home.

They had their successes. Even the incumbent of the cathedral church, a worthy man, confessed later to claiming a new Christian confidence and sense of personal trust in the Lord.

There were practical issues to attend to. The first was the change into Chinese clothing. The men had expected this and were ready for it. Even so, they felt at first slightly ridiculous as they set aside their well-tailored European clothes for the long wide skirts, loose overjackets with wide sleeves, thick calico stockings and flat padded shoes. They knew that in really cold weather they would add more padded clothing. Charley wrote home, 'I have been laughing all day at our grotesque appearance.' Heads had to be shaved and a piece of hair at the back of the head plaited into a long pigtail known as a queue or *bianzi*. This, with the extension of a piece of black silk cord, hung right down the back.

Thus attired, they stalked about feeling odd at first – seven highly athletic young men, used to striding out, hurling cricket balls, using their arms for vigorous rowing. Their new dress seemed to indicate a more restrained form of movement, through the sheer weight of the garments. They supposed they would soon get used to the new clothing. They soon thought nothing about it at all, except that it was very comfortable.

And they became accustomed to the missionary ladies in their demure long robes, walking very quietly and slowly and, if married, often behind their husbands. 'The etiquette with ladies is very strict here', wrote home Stanley Smith. But the European ladies within their Chinese robes were quite tough in their witness. The use of women missionaries was considered quite daring and advanced but they had proved most valuable. There were delightful married ladies like Mrs Hudson Taylor, Jennie, known by the Chinese as 'Miss Happiness', and also, the young men noted, some lovely missionary girls just out from England.

The matter of their personal finances arose privately between Hudson Taylor and the seven. Probably all the young men had private incomes, some good allowances, and some knew that in a year or two they would inherit large fortunes. They felt that this was unscriptural and a hindrance and that they should get rid of their money and offer it to Hudson for the mission. Charley Studd knew that at twenty-five he would inherit vast wealth. Hudson persuaded him to forget about this until the time came. But Charley knew that then he would be giving it away, which he did when the time came. He was an impulsive creature and always would be.

The seven were warmly welcomed by the existing missionaries of the CIM and began to realise that much good work was going on and had been long before their coming. The CIM stood out because of its unique principles, but there were by now other missionary societies working in China. Few, if any, felt that they should or could try to penetrate the China vastnesses as Hudson Taylor had always intended to do.

The seven began to realise the true size of the Chinese Empire. In his book *China's Spiritual Needs and Claims*, Hudson explained to readers the huge nature of this mysterious part of the globe. The area, he said, was altogether 5,300,000 square miles – forty-four times the size of the United Kingdom and Ireland. At that time, he wrote, 'Chinese Tartary and Tibet contain rather more than three-fifths, the remaining two-fifths being contained in China proper.'

The seven began to understand more of the struggles of the early days of the mission and of the extreme difficulties in those days of leaving the five Treaty ports and trying to go inland. The Chinese – who considered themselves to be the centre of the world ('The Middle Kingdom') – had never wished to have anything to do with 'foreign devils' and had resisted fiercely attempts to form bonds or trade with foreign powers. When they did so, it was under duress. The 'opium wars' had not shown Britain at her best and there had always been much resentment at foreign intervention.

But Hudson, in his mission, had determined that Christ should be brought to all of China's millions if possible, since he believed that without the knowledge and opportunity of salvation they had no hope. So he and his followers had daringly entered forbidden territories and in a quiet way offered Christ.

And now, 1885, was a time of 'open doors' in the great Empire when a period of gospel expansion was planned. The seven came to appreciate the faithful work carried out by former missionaries, most of whom had few of the advantages of the seven. In unspectacular ways the CIM and others preached night and morning in street chapels, visited homes and received guests, or tramped doggedly through the provinces scattering leaflets. They were courageous and devoted.

The seven recognised that they had not come to 'save' the mission but to add their gifts, their health and strength and dedication to a mission already bursting with power. They would make good friends and companions over the years and some would find wives among the missionary women who were now a most respected feature of the mission staff. The seven were just seven among forty missionaries newly arrived and it was a thrilling time.

But they had a lot to learn and they knew that the most essential was a mastery of the Chinese language. The Chinese do not have an alphabet as we do; the characters called ideographs are more like pictures, each picture meaning the same to any Chinese, just as an Englishman and a Frenchman can both understand the picture of a cow. The Chinese have only two written forms and anyone in China can write meaningfully to anyone else. But the spoken form has many dialects, which adds to the difficulty of mastering the speech.

In the end, all would master this task. They realised that without any smattering of the language, they could make little progress. They muttered to one another that they hated being 'silent and dumb'. They longed to be able to pass on their message of hope as they had been doing so effectively for the past year or two at home. Hudson Taylor would be doing something about their ignorance.

Hudson had his own definite plans for the company. In expanding situations, he bore huge responsibilities but he wanted to make the most of the gift of the seven he had acquired. His plan was that they should eventually pioneer the great province of Szechwan, apart from the river region between the already occupied cities. It was a rich and populous province and ripe for the Gospel.

He saw no problem in the men working together. It was his custom to put together people of the same branch of the Christian Church if possible, and the seven were all nominally Anglican. Willie Cassels and young Arthur Polhill-Turner were devout Anglicans and wanted to plant the Anglican Church firmly on the soil of China.

But Hudson simply could not send seven

young Englishmen, however disguised in Chinese clothing, together to travel in one group. It just would not do. The men so obviously stood out from the smaller Chinese around them. They all looked so buoyantly healthy and physically active. Moreover, both Cecil Polhill-Turner and Dick Hoste bore a military bearing as befitted ex-soldiers that was unmistakable and might perhaps seem to threaten the Chinese. Hudson was sure the seven would never all get a pass to travel together in this way, and he explained this to them.

So he split them into two groups of three. Studd and Smith were separated as their mothers had decided they were too impulsive and excitable to travel together. And as Lady Beauchamp had implored, for the time being Hudson kept Monty with him.

The mothers of the seven were influential and remarkable women and their sons loved and admired them. But the time had come for them to be free of parental supervision and to live as men among men. Mrs Studd had always fussed over Charley, even sending on extra clothing when he had made a hasty departure for a rally. Mrs Smith had pestered Jennie Taylor to know what the young missionaries needed; all kinds of tableware and niceties were sent out to China to be rather brushed off by the recipients. The seven were determined to live simply and to put lives of luxury behind them.

So Charley and the Polhill brothers, in the care of John McCarthy as escort/interpreter, were sent up the river Yangtze to Hankow, 700 miles in four days by steamer and then up the river Han to Hanchung by river boat.

'It was a thousand miles in four months', wrote Charley, 'and those the hottest of the year, real baking weather, but the Lord kept us in good health. We had grand times together, reading the word and praying.' Someone remarked that they were 'Three Etonians on a river picnic!' Perhaps they sang the Eton boating song . . . .

Meanwhile, Stanley, Dick and Willie went on a longish sea voyage via Yantai to Tianjin, thence through Peking to Shanxi. Here they were to get down to their Chinese study and work alongside the famous Chinese Pastor Hsi.

Chapter 5

The Real Test

'We had our wilderness journey but the wilderness blossomed like the rose,' Charley Studd said. The long water journey to Hanchung was full of interest for the travellers. Their native boat on the river Han had three compartments, quite adequate, but the boat travelled very slowly, thirty miles a day was good going. 'It certainly teaches us patience', said Charley. This was evidently a quality needed in China where nobody seemed to hurry. This would not be easy for Charley.

He was alert to everything new. 'The Chinese are not idle', he wrote home. 'The coolies carry loads of up to 224 lbs., and stick at things till they are done. They have plenty of "backbone". When they are converted they make splendid Christians. They endure so much hardship in their lives.' He noted how provident they were. 'The Chinese will make the most of every inch of ground and waste no time. As soon as one crop is gathered, they will plant something else.'

Arthur was impressed by the open nature of the society as they were then experiencing it. 'You can go into nearly every heathen temple in the land and preach for as long as you like and the priest will come and listen. In some parts, temples have been converted to places of Christian worship.'

The young men had to get used to Chinese currency. The only coin in circulation was called 'a cash', a brass coin with a square hole in it. Twenty–five cash made up 'one penny'. They were amused and somewhat dismayed to find that they had to take on board for the entire journey over half a ton of brass coin, threaded in thousands on strings, about half a million cash altogether. 'It sounds a great deal', laughed Charley, 'but really the whole journey of 1,800 miles won't cost much more than £10 a head – everything included.'

They rippled past beautiful and varied country, though rather short of foliage. Every now and then they saw a valley between the hills and a picturesque cottage and farm embedded in trees of the loveliest hue of the light green leaves of early summer. They noticed that the houses had curly roofs rather like the Swiss chalets they had seen on holidays.

They were impressed by the splendid river Han, sometimes miles across, covered with junks of all kinds. When they stopped, they had to get used to the insatiable curiosity of the Chinese. 'They crowd round us with curious eyes and ask the most absurd questions. They want to know about our "exalted age", our wives and children, and whether the sun ever shines in our country.' This was nothing to what the women missionaries had to put up with. When these ladies wore black stockings, they were often asked 'if they had white arms and black legs . . .'

In May, Arthur noticed how beautiful the waving corn was, the mountains and the cloudless blue sky. 'Praise the Lord', he found himself crying.

By June they reached Hing-Ngan where they changed boats. Here a painful incident occurred when they anchored in a quiet cove in the mountains where, alas, the water was very swift. Some decided to bathe in the extreme heat. A native Christian servant, Liao, was suddenly carried away by the force of the current. Cecil, who was standing by, though fully clothed, plunged into the water and tried to save poor Liao, but so heavy were his garments and so rapid the water, it was impossible. They were all very upset that Liao was drowned.

In July, Arthur wrote home that 'the Chinese are a very clever race and most ingenious'. He noted how early they got up in the morning and how hard they worked. He saw, while ashore, a Mandarin (a provincial governor) making a tour of the city in his sedan chair, preceded by a loud gong.

By August they had arrived in Hanchung, in the province of Shen-si. They were glad to get there, having become rather weary of their language study and the slow pace of their travelling. They quickly got into working stride, struggling with their Chinese and making a Christian witness publicly whenever they could. Arthur thought that a good way of improving their Chinese was to mingle more with the native peoples. He and his brother went every morning therefore into the dispensary to pick up useful new words. As the months passed, and they learned some useful phrases, they began to evangelise, and were quite pleased with the results. An old-fashioned love feast was held, 'with tea and cakes, hymns and speeches'.

* * * * * *

Meanwhile, the second party of the seven had taken their long journey by water through the Yellow Sea and the Gulf of Peh-chi-hi. Disembarking, they were greeted by a small group of English people in Tianjin where they met with great kindness. Then on to Peking which they reached in May. Stanley Smith's eloquence was valuable in encouraging the missionaries and their families working there. They could get downhearted sometimes. Stanley was improving with his Chinese vocabulary. His immediate efforts were to get the Chinese to destroy their idols. One of the resident missionaries declared 'a tide of revival is beating on the Chinese shore'.

Sometimes they saw victory. On the first and fifteenth of each month, the Chinese had a grand worshipping of idols. They went early in the morning to the temples to sacrifice fowls and burn incense, and also lighted candles at home. One day, an eldest son asked the *po-po* (grandmother) if he should burn the incense as usual and she replied: 'No, I don't believe in that now. I believe in the true God'. So no idols were worshipped there that day or since. The people saved up their incense money to build a chapel where the Gospel could be preached. This was their own idea.

The party toured the amazing city of Peking, with its Great Wall and the famous Ming tombs. They visited the temple of Confucius which covered a wide area, completely walled round. It was powerfully built and well maintained. In the great hall were tablets in which the spirits of departed great ones were supposed to reside. This was an honoured shrine for the Chinese.

Willie Cassels was looking forward to some 'seclusion' in Ping-Yang where he could push on with the language. He had an eye for nature and observed with interest, in June, the young maize and, of course, the opium poppy. 'It looks very beautiful', he wrote, 'but alas the moral aspect of this plant is anything but lovely.' The poppy was, of course, the source of heroin. The plant was increasingly cultivated in that area and yet, shamefully, the Chinese frequently spoke of it as 'the foreign plant' because of British involvement in the opium trade. Willie was saddened by this.

In the Ho-chau area he was delighted by the native birds – 'so wonderfully tame'. He saw magpies and pigeons hopping along the road and he had heard of an eagle swooping down to take a piece of meat from a man's hand. He enjoyed the free approach of the fearless birds, but also remembered that wolves from the hills nearby also sometimes grew bold and attacked travellers and their mules on the roadside.

* * * * * *

The inns at which the party stayed varied in standards of comfort and cleanliness but were never too awful to put up with. Sleeping was on a *Kiang* – a heated brick platform bed – not soft but warm and cosy. Surprisingly quickly they became accustomed to the food, plenty of fresh vegetables and eating with chopsticks. And when they had to 'rough it' they did so uncomplainingly. Said Willie: 'A little acquaintance with flies, mosquitoes and other animals of worse description does one good and is only what travellers in inns may expect!'

Travelling could be painful, jolting about on muleback, carts being expensive. The mules made Willie laugh. 'The first thing they do when they get to the inn in the evening is to lie down and have a good roll in the dust; sometimes they do this on the journey when we stop for a few moments. The carters just look on and smile.'

As Willie and Stanley rode on and approached Ping-Yang, a Chinese man ran up and thrust out his hand. Stanley at once realised that the man must be a Christian, as he made the Christian salute – a deep bow with the two closed hands placed together in front and then brought up to the forehead. So Stanley asked him *'Yiae-su- mun-tu*?' (Are you a disciple of Jesus?). The man smiled, nodded and shook hands. Stanley thought – 'This is the first time I have shaken hands with a Chinaman.' The man then invited them to have refreshments by the roadside and gave them bread and rice-water. 'I have been praying that missionaries might come', he told the interpreter. The man went along with them and as they drew near to his town, he said, 'All the people here are giving up their idols.' Stanley and Willie gave a cheer.

At last they reached Ping-Yang Fu. This was an ancient city which had been the residence of the Emperor in 2,000 BC. Here they hoped for three months hard study. Stanley did not think the language was as hard as he had expected, but he had perhaps a special gift for it. 'You can get along with two or three thousand characters', he decided. Like all the others in this strange land, he prayed for patience.

They found the two adjoining houses belonging to the mission, where there was plenty of room for them, and Stanley wrote home, 'The house has been roughly whitewashed. The four of us – Monty, Dick, Willie and I – occupy three sides of a little courtyard, each having a room to himself. The brick-bed arrangements, under which a fire can be lighted in the winter, have been removed as they take up a great deal of room. My bed is an unused door, stretched across the two short forms we found, and I assure you it makes a capital bedstead. If you know anyone who wants to set up house cheaply – let them try this! And when we get inside the courtyard, it is nice and cool . . . .'

Their escort, Frederick Baller, found them a teacher and they settled down to benefit from his instruction. When the hard hours of study were over, usually seven hours a day, they stretched themselves and strolled on the city walls, with fine views of the distant mountains and the setting sun. They were at peace with themselves.

* * * * * *

When Charley's party faced the long overland journey to join up with their friends in Ping-Yang Fu, this proved a tough physical test, especially for soft western feet. Charley's feet had been fine on the cricket field but here they were required to go very briskly for long periods of time over very rough ground. He soon discarded his uncomfortable new Chinese shoes, and very soon even the coolie straw sandals that he tried next. Finally, he was marching on bare blistered feet and in great pain. The colporteurs who carried the Bible packs wanted to hurry on, to do as much as forty miles per day. 'Each step was like a knife', admitted Charley later. But he was determined not to get behind. As one foot became infected and swollen, he asked a companion that night to anoint him with oil and pray especially for him. It seems that from the following morning, the foot improved and the swelling went down. Charley was a great believer in the value of the biblical practice of anointing with oil.

Chapter 6

Problems and Answers

Dick Hoste decided to go off by himself and spend some time in Huh-Wu Hien. Mr Baller rented a plain little house for him and Dick engaged a language teacher for himself. 'I feel a step further into the fight,' he said and went about distributing books in the surrounding villages and doing his best with his limited Chinese.

'The villages here are more than half depopulated', he wrote home, 'and broken-down houses, ruined walls and neglected roadways and bridges, all speak of a departed prosperity.' But the people were working hard to make improvements, growing tobacco, cotton and millet.

Monty, still at Ping-Yang, was fascinated by everything. He had pity for the Chinese who felt the need for inward peace but did not know how to find it. 'I have met some who are very rigid and self-righteous', he said. 'One said he had not eaten onions, garlic, eggs or meat of any kind, nor taken tobacco, but he knew nothing of the peace of the Lord Jesus.'

The useless superstitions of the people distressed all the missionaries. Monty heard a tale of a special ceremony performed for a man because his business was in bad shape.

A missionary had been called to witness this event, which began with a great noise of beating gongs and blowing of trumpets. Round the man's house were arranged several raised tables, each with candles and incense burning and bearing a large coloured house made of paper. There were also effigies of ancestors and cardboard tablets with ancestors' names. By the side of the tables were bonfires of paper – supposed to resemble paper money – and this was to go to the ancestors. Priests chanted and wailed and an old priest in scarlet satin robes was in charge. The eldest member of the man's family stood at the priest's right hand. All along the street at intervals they placed lighted candles to light the spirits of their ancestors. This ceremony went on for hours – it was carried out to satisfy the spirits of the ancestors.

'Isn't it terribly sad,' said the missionary. 'You will now understand something of the superstition and darkness that reign here. We pray that the Light may soon dispel the darkness.'

* * * * * *

The party went to visit the famous Pastor Hsi, a

former Confucian scholar, a man of some small private means who, when he was converted, had lost his official rank – or his 'button' as it was called. This fine Christian man was well-known for the opium refuges he had founded. He said that 'God had taught him the secret of making opium pills which help to alleviate the pain of those who have given up the terrible drug and he therefore kept the secret to himself and by the sale of those pills he earned a livelihood.'

Hudson Taylor was up to his ears with decision-making. The tide of progress running so rapidly brought its own problems. Snippets of disquieting news came about the Cambridge Seven. He heard that Charley Studd and the Polhill brothers were being difficult about their Chinese lessons. Charley had decided that this tedious studying of the language was too slow a method. Surely, he argued, if they prayed to God for the gift of this particular tongue, it would be a better idea. He persuaded the Polhills that this might be so and also two rather impressionable young missionary women at Hanchung. Mercifully, before the autumn ended, they had decided that this was all a stupid mistake and had returned to the discipline of their books.

Hudson raised his eyes to the ceiling. He would always say to new missionaries – 'If I could put the Chinese language into your brains by one wave of the hand, I would not do it.' He knew that unadapted foreign thought and idiom merely translated into Chinese would do little good. Months of submission to a Chinese scholar while watching and listening to evangelists and experienced missionaries taught wisdom as well as language.

He next got the hint from the other 'seven' party that Frederick Baller, leader and guide of that group, was 'keeping a very tight rein' on his new charges. Dick Hoste had written very carefully and without a real protest, but Hudson could see that Baller was being 'too bossy' for mature men. Also, instead of Baller finding new fellowship in the company, he had reported to Hudson Taylor that he was repelled by the extreme piety of Stanley and Dick and felt that their times of prayer and fasting were excessive. Hudson realised that the two men were still in the early stages of their commitment to the new cause and were perhaps 'going over the top'.

'How many and subtle are the devices', sighed Hudson, 'to keep the Chinese ignorant of the Gospel.'

Also, Pastor Hsi, an outstanding man but one of a rather fiery temper, was not the easiest person to work with. Life was not easy for Hudson.

Of course, the Cambridge Seven were no longer 'golden boys' whose every word and move was hung upon. They were having to learn to adapt to circumstances and to fit in with the life of the mission. In their enthusiasm, they sometimes made mistakes. Cassels and Beauchamp were sent by themselves to open a new centre west of the Fen river at Sichau. They felt hopelessly inexperienced and lost. Willie Cassels was now better at understanding what Chinese people said, Monty Beauchamp at making himself understood. They clung together in their work as 'ears' and 'mouth'. It was understandable that they sometimes felt a bit depressed. It was often very hard to start up new stations. The Mandarin might imprison a landlord who let to foreigners. And some Chinese believed that anyone who drank tea in a foreigner's house would go mad.

Sometimes they witnessed lively Chinese customs that interested them and gave them food for thought. One such was the festival of the Dragon Feast. This began on 1st June and continued for three days. On the third day, the shops were all closed and everyone went down to the river where there were a great number of boats in the shape of a dragon. Gongs were sounded and fireworks let off. They understood that this festival was instituted in memory of a Chinese statesman who was drowned in the river. There was much racing of the boats backwards and forwards on the river as if searching for the spirit of the dead man. A feast was then held at which it was correct to give and receive presents, one of these being a rice cake.

Another interesting festival was Chinese New Year, when most people seemed not to go to bed at all. There was feasting and wine drinking and the letting off of fireworks to frighten away evil spirits. So, at this time, the Christians decided to hold a midnight service of praise and prayer.

The missionaries realised that the Chinese people were very superstitious and always attributed sudden death to the influence of evil spirits. If a foreigner was there, it must be his or her fault.

* * * * * *

From Sichau they moved round the surrounding villages and small towns. They found that in Taning, a little city nestling among the hills, some Christian groundwork had been carried out by a former Buddhist priest and a Chinese scholar. There were twenty-two Christians already there and the men received a never-ending stream of callers, fascinated by their English Bible and their English pens and pencils.

Then some persecution arose in Taning, when officials friendly to the Faith were replaced by others. Serious charges were levelled at the Christians, including Willie Cassels, the most inoffensive of men, who, it was asserted, had destroyed an idol in the Buddhist temple. Willie found his own house barred to him and threatening, stamping mobs around. He could do nothing useful there at that moment, so he forded a river in a storm to reach the safety of a Chinese friend's house, where he stayed until it seemed prudent to return. Back in Taning he levered the barred door of his home off its hinges and boldly marched in. Within three months a new Mandarin was installed, the Chinese returned to their friendly ways and things again went happily.

Then back to Sichau. Monty Beauchamp described to friends how they were making some progress through the use of three large wall-texts which he had got written out in Chinese characters in Ping-Yang. These they stuck up in their reception room and could point at them when their own Chinese vocabulary ran out. The texts were: 'Matthew chapter 11, verse 28 – 'Come to me all whose work is hard, whose load is heavy and I will give you relief.' The second was the Epistle to the Romans, chapter 5, verse 8: 'Christ died for us while we were yet sinners', and the third, the Book of Hebrews, chapter 7 verse 25: 'He is able to save absolutely those who approach God through Him.' Gradually, the merely inquisitive and the sight-seers dropped off and only those came who were really seekers after truth.

Willie and Monty faced the real tragedy of the opium takers and their sad lives. Monty told a friend: 'About 80 per cent of the people in this neighbourhood smoke opium; it's much worse than the horrors of drink.' Where people had miserable lives, including women and young girls, the addiction was fairly understandable but this did not help. Monty felt embarrassed since it was well-known that the British were in so large a part responsible for this awful habit. He said: 'It used to be only an indulgence for the wealthy, on whom it was less harmful as they had plenty of food at the same time; now it is grown here everywhere by everybody and people will get it by hook or crook.'

Monty went on: 'After the Chinese war the British forced the Indian opium trade on China against the strongest opposition. Eventually the Chinese took to growing it themselves – can you blame them?' He felt he would not have been surprised if the Chinese had refused ever to listen to any gospel brought from Britain. The plight of the addicts with their dreadful cravings really upset him.

'One man's face I shall never forget. He begged us to open a refuge. I was obliged to say I could do nothing then for him, only recommend him to the Great Physician, Jesus. If every mission station would open an opium refuge, a great work could be done.' It was a dark and bitter struggle.

Chapter 7

Years of Achievement

From then until the year 1900, the seven continued to develop Christian work in China. They would obediently go where sent but they appreciated the freedom with which their service was accepted. If they felt they had a particular skill for some area and could use it there, they were free to go there. Much of their success depended upon their various personalities which by now, as they approached maturity, were more clearly defined.

There were the 'quiet ones', reliable and not bothered by repetitious duties and slow building up of little congregations. Dick Hoste and Arthur Polhill-Turner might be said to be of this nature. For ten years Arthur made his sphere in Pachow, where he worked happily on routine station duties. He was ordained as an Anglican clergyman in 1888. Later he moved to other bases in the province of North Szechwan, working in the thickly populated countryside. He soon found a nice young bride to work with him.

Dick would go off alone, as to Ping-Yang, from time to time, but basically worked with Pastor Hsi in Hung Tung until the pastor died. Greater responsibilities awaited him. He seemed able to find the inner resources to work with the fiery Pastor, something that others found difficult. Dick had sat down and thought about the pastor's earlier life and realised why he behaved in the rather autocratic manner he adopted. The pastor had never, for one thing, had any traditional missionary training.

An unpleasant incident caused by rivalry and jealousy put the pastor in danger of his life. It was a long time before all this calmed down and friendly relationships in the area were resumed. This made the pastor more humble and easier for Dick to get on with. 'We just grew together,' said Dick simply. It was obvious that Dick had great powers of leadership and great pastoral powers too. He had, of course, begun his adult life as an Army officer and was accustomed to making decisions and giving orders. But he kept forcefulness in check and was a wise and loving person beyond his years. This was all noticed by the keen-eyed Hudson Taylor.

Stanley Smith was ebullient and lively, always cheerful and ready to speak for the Lord. He didn't find it difficult to make contact with people. 'You have no idea how fascinating the village work is', he told his friends. 'You go out to a village and just sit down by a group. The people are keen to hear and very friendly. Very shortly "the cup that cheers but not inebriates" is brought and while you drink the tea you have the fullest opportunity of telling the story which always seems the better for telling – the story of the Cross.'

Stanley worked busily in the northern town of Hung Tung. He was enthusiastic at giving out Christian leaflets, but even more on sticking them up on walls where they could be read by crowds. 'We use the paste-pot a good deal,' he wrote, 'and on a small scale these leaflets posted on walls and available places remind me of the advertisement for Coleman's mustard! It is my firm belief that one tract wisely pasted, is worth ten given away . . . ' He and Monty Beauchamp had 'attacked' the town of Hung Tung, taking leaflets to every shop, selling many cash worth of books, and buttonholing little groups and talking to them. Stanley liked to sing and told of gathering some lads together on a Sunday afternoon to 'sing to them of Jesus'. He could always draw people to him. Said Dick of him, years later: 'He was a brilliant, most attractive fellow.'

Willie Cassels said goodbye to the province of Shanyi and moved on to the area which was set apart by Hudson Taylor for Church of England missionaries, and which was to be Willie's home for the rest of his life. He travelled for a month with a Chinese boy servant, across the

Yellow River, which was known as 'China's sorrow' because of its frequent terrible floods. He crossed the vast Sian plain and then entered rough and rocky mountainous countryside to reach Hanchung, his starting point for entry into the western region of Szechwan. Throughout this journey, he did not pass a single mission station. And away to the north west was the great province of Gansu, which with Chinese Turkestan extends into the very heart of Asia, with just four stations and three of these only newly opened. In Szechwan itself, a province of 60,000,000 people, there were then only two mission stations. No wonder Hudson Taylor was concerned. He designated the densely populated area of Eastern Szechwan as a 'China Inland Mission Church of England sphere'. Here Willie Cassels would in time make a name for himself but, above all, make known the name of Jesus Christ. Willie was sometimes joined in his work there by Arthur and Monty.

Szechwan was the largest province in China and had boundless natural resources, oil and salt wells, beside magnificent waterways, massive mountains and many temple and rock carvings. Willie set his heart on Paoning, later to be known as Lanzhong, and here he held high the cross of Christ.

Paoning was the most important prefectural city in North Szechwan. It held official status and sometimes as many as 10,000 students flocked to the city for the examinations. Huge crowds also came for the festivals. The city itself was noted for its vinegar, and nearby the famous Chinese silk was produced. Picturesque Paoning stood on the banks of the Jailin river, almost encircled by the river and surrounded by hills. The lanes in the suburbs were quite English-looking and stirred Willie's feelings.

Things were not easy at first. 'We were suspected and distrusted,' wrote Willie. 'Our knowledge of the language was still small and no house could at first be purchased or rented.'

He turned to prayer and after much aggravation finally found somewhere to live. Before long, a charming and spirited girl, a worker from his former Lambeth parish, appeared on the missionary scene and soon they were married in the cathedral in Shanghai. Willie had found a true helpmate in Mary Louisa and she certainly needed courage to enter her new life in Paoning. No foreign woman had ever gone there before so she was naturally apprehensive as they travelled home by Chinese houseboat through the frightening Yangtze gorges. They reached Paoning in January 1888. 'We entered stealthily at night, fearing to create alarm.' A strange beginning to married life for this new bride! Soon crowds began to appear. She was prepared for this, but it was unnerving. It was not nice to be stared at so unblinkingly and then to have personal remarks directed at you. 'Why is your skin so white?' 'Why is your hair the colour of a cow?' Poor Mary Louisa. But she was a young woman of spirit and stood up well to the difficulties.

At the time of the Dragon Festival the crowds surged in and Willie was forced to erect partitions across the rooms to protect his wife. But she soon settled into her new life and began to enjoy it. She liked to wander in the lanes nearby where the hedges were bursting with violets and other less familiar wild flowers. She liked to sit to read in her little paved courtyard. She was a great help to Willie and they were particularly busy when the students crowded the city. Monty Beauchamp paid them a visit and was soon involved in the work. He wrote home: 'It was real hard work, needing all my strength. The scholars kept us at work from morn to night, and almost all who came were presented with a book and tract, while several hundred Gospels were also given away.'

Mary Louisa was always discovering new and interesting facts about the Chinese way of life. One of the lady workers at Paoning told of having been invited to a ceremony for the little baby of some Chinese neighbours, the Iangs. The infant was one year old and the ceremony was to decide about his future. Mary Louisa learned that three tables covered with red cloth were set up in the middle of the room and on these were placed clothes, books, pens, lamps, gambling boards, cakes, an abacus and other articles. The baby was put into a space in the middle. It was thought that whatever the baby first grabbed at would influence his life thereafter. If he picked up a book, he would be a scholar. If he snatched at a lamp, he would go into trade and make money. How great were the cultural gaps, thought Mary Louisa.

Her husband, Willie Cassels, was soon accepted as a natural leader and was very proud of being an ordained priest of the Church of England. He was a person who liked things to be orderly and insisted that the liturgical life of the Church should be carried out properly. He was also someone who liked to receive clear instructions from those above him and to 'keep to the rules'. So he pursued an even life and those around him knew what to expect.

At seven in the morning, Willie held Chinese prayers, followed by a meeting with the opium patients who, sadly, formed a large part of all the visitors to the mission. He gave out medicines and also explained the basic truths of the Gospel. At dusk came enquirers who must be answered. On Sundays there were services and prayer-meetings to try to influence those still bowing to idols. There were, gloriously, sometimes Christian baptisms to be carried out and not always on babies. There was Li, the son of a Chinese teacher; Wen, an old man who kept a hat shop; another Li who was a shoemaker, and

Ku-Holin, a young Muhammadan boy who later became a Christian Archdeacon.

It was all very thrilling. In just one year, thought Willie, they had got not just one house but four and now eleven missionaries were working in and from Paoning.

Occasionally there occurred what Willie described as 'a little diversion of some of the people', meaning 'trouble' – 'the annoyance of the devil at the good hearing given to the Gospel.'

This once involved Mary Louisa who had gone to visit the village of Chen-ia-pa with a Biblewoman. It was too far to return the same day and she had to stay the night. She visited a women's court where great interest and excitement was shown. She finally retired to sleep but was abruptly awakened by a great noise at the large doors. 'All the household got up in great alarm and came to my door, begging me to get up quickly and dress. They wanted me to go and hide on the other side of the court. My Biblewoman soon got dressed but I did not get up – I felt sure that the Lord would protect me and not allow the mob to get in. Though I was suffering from palpitation of the heart and oppressed by a heavy cold, I was very happy and did not feel in the least afraid, for the Lord kept me in perfect peace.' The crowd dispersed and Mary Louisa was safe.

The following year the young couple had a baby girl, Jessie. Mary Louisa was at first puzzled since the Chinese seemed sad for them. She soon found that the Chinese were anxious to bear boy babies and did not think much of having girls. In fact, in those days, girl babies were sometimes left to perish on the mountainsides. So the young Cassels parents were glad to be able to show to all their deep joy at baby Jessie and they gave a feast in her honour. They showed some magic-lantern slides which astonished the viewers, who had never seen anything like that before.

As little Jessie grew, Mary Louisa took her about and demonstrated the joy of the young parents in this lovely child. When Jessie was a few years old, she was taken along to a great missionary conference held in Shanghai and ran happily about among the delegates.

Sometimes Mary Louisa had to stay alone in Paoning whilst Willie was travelling, and these trips sometimes occurred during seasons of riots, which came and went for no real reason. She wrote to her husband, 'I went to the street daily and took little Jessie with me and the people were friendly . . . we mix with them as much as we can.' That year, in the early months, they had fifteen baptisms in Paoning and the work grew rapidly.

There was much pleasure at the conversion of an adopted son of the family Wang. This lad had lived a wild and reckless life, having been dismissed from his regiment for smoking opium. He went back to his home and sought peace through Buddhism and Confucianism. At last he found his way to the mission station in Paoning and was eventually baptised in the Name of the Lord Jesus.

Troubles flared up on the smallest pretext and then, as quickly, died down. In one moment of such crisis, Willie found Chinese people stirred up against him and they marched to the mission and forcibly removed the roof. Unperturbed, Willie slept on. When it rained, he put up an umbrella over his bed and slept with a waterproof sheet over him. He refused to be put out of his home again. He was building a new chapel in Paoning and nothing was going to stop him.

Chapter 8

The Adventurers

All the Cambridge Seven were now able to make themselves understood in their adopted language and had acquired the competence to travel anywhere and carry out missionary work by themselves. But while some opened new stations and stayed to build them up, others found it more natural and profitable to itinerate – that is to take the long, hard journeys to places where no one before had ever gone with the message of the Gospel.

Among these were Monty Beauchamp and Cecil Polhill-Turner. They were both men of strong physique and the necessary stamina, able to walk for miles when required, to take care of themselves in difficult situations without causing an international incident, and not easily overcome by problems or dismayed by loneliness. Cecil, as an ex-Guards officer, was a person of initiative and was fascinated by the amazing country to which they had given their lives. He found himself drawn to the mysterious untouched area of Tibet, that secretive land in the extreme north-west of China. This was a 'forbidden' area where no foreigners were acceptable and it remained largely that way, as it does yet.

Tibet is sometimes called 'the roof of the world' since it holds the highest mountain mass in the world, the Himalaya range. It is rich in mineral resources with gold in its river beds and turquoise in its mines.

Cecil understood that the religion of the Tibetans was 'Lamaism' – a strange mixture of Buddhism, sorcery and certain old Hindu beliefs. There were numerous monasteries and monks in the country and any education that existed was in the hands of the monks. At the time when Cecil began his march towards Tibet, it had closed its frontiers. To get into it, or anywhere near it, was definitely a challenge.

Many Tibetans lived in the neighbouring province of Gansu and there, on the edges of Tibet, Cecil had some successes and made friends with Tibetans. He also talked to travellers about the ruler of Tibet, the Dalai Lama, who lived in a famous monastery. Cecil was most anxious to make contact with this gentleman. Cecil had always moved in high social circles and was not at all bothered by the thought of meeting such a lofty figure and trying to make a way for the Gospel.

Equal with him in daring and initiative was

Monty Beauchamp, a giant of a man, tough and resilient. Monty loved the hard travelling life, not stopping long in one place but always moving on, always challenged by the call to a further outpost. He was a true evangelist, needing to carry very little equipment or goods with him, trusting the Lord for sustenance and unafraid of any situation.

Through a set of family circumstances, when Monty finally inherited the family title and the family seat, there was not much inheritance to go with it. But he had been quite prepared, as he had explained privately earlier to Hudson Taylor, to renounce the family fortune of probably a quarter of a million pounds, which he had expected to inherit.

Monty made a memorable journey with Hudson Taylor himself as companion and this was a tour of nearly 1,000 miles, from Shanxi to Hanchung. It was a trip with considerable hazards and Monty never forgot it. They had to cross the great Yellow River and since this was running high and very dangerous, they nearly came to grief. The ferry was overloaded with carts, mules and passengers squashed together, and in the strong current it began to roll as they were swept downstream. Then several mules toppled overboard and swam. Equilibrium was restored and they safely reached the further shore.

Monty was much impressed by Hudson

Taylor's calm demeanour, especially since Hudson was considerably older than himself. Monty was struck by Hudson's powers of endurance and the fact that, no matter how awkward the situation or rough the surroundings, Hudson was 'always the same man with the same spirit, with food, without it, with rest, without it.'

Because Hudson felt the heat so much he preferred to travel at night. So he on a mule and Monty on foot pushed on and reached their destination before others in the party. Monty found night travelling hard, especially since he found it difficult to sleep in the daytime. Hudson was aware of this and tried to make things easier for him, rigging up a mosquito net to keep the flies off. Sometimes they would spend a night in an inn and when Monty woke early to feed the mules before daylight, he would always find Hudson already awake, reading his Bible by candlelight. Sometimes they slept by the roadside – they each carried two pillows, one for the shoulder, one for the thigh, and a blanket to cover themselves with. To Monty and Hudson, these things did not matter much, creature comforts were no problem. It was Monty's pleasure to be able to help sometimes when fording the flooded rivers. Waist-deep in the strong streams, he would easily carry Hudson's slight form on his powerful shoulders. This long journey taught Monty much; it was splendid experience and above all, from Hudson's cheerful, prayerful manner, Monty learned about valuable attitudes when travelling.

He was now free to choose his ministry and he opted for long 'colportages' – tours through the towns and villages taking Bibles to those who had never heard the Gospel story. He was by now competent in Chinese and people liked to hear him preach. He made long journeys through Henan to Shanxi and back to Szechwan and another to the remote province of Gansu. Finally, he chose to concentrate on Gansu. He became among the most experienced and knowledgeable of the younger workers of the CIM. He grew to love the Chinese people and was paid a compliment by the Consul at Wanxian who said that Monty was so devoted to the Chinese that he was 'at the beck and call of any coolie'. This is how Monty wished it to be.

* * * * * *

The other 'adventurer' of the seven was Charley Studd, very much an individualist and one who found it more difficult to work with others and to await instructions. An attractive, impulsive person, Charley feared no foe but often did not do a great deal of consulting. He had, for example, his own very definite views upon the matter of his personal fortune. He had volunteered, in 1886, to go down to Chunking with a companion to see if any rescues could be effected during a time of riots. Murder, burning and looting had taken place and foreigners were definitely unsafe. Charley was not afraid of anything and willingly slipped off and found a way into Chunking. His appearance surprised the only person he found, a rather nervous consul, not anxious to entertain any foreigners. But while there, Charley was able to carry out a plan he had held in mind for several years – to give away his personal fortune. In spite of protests, he insisted upon the Consul witnessing his signature to deeds which parted him from the considerable monies that he now inherited at the age of twenty-five. Charley was determined. He was going to be no rich young ruler! So he arranged for large sums to go to Moody's work in North India, to George Müller of Bristol for work among the orphans; to charities among the London poor and to the Salvation Army in India. He also wrote big cheques for General Booth, Dr Barnardo, the CIM, and the poor of Dublin. After all this was settled, he found he still had £3,400 left.

Soon after this happening, Charley met the young lady he was to marry, Priscilla Livingstone Stewart. He decided to give her the remainder of his fortune. She, in turn, decided to pass this amount to the Salvation Army. Charley felt he was now free of the worry of his money. He believed this was a scriptural way to behave and Priscilla agreed with him.

Priscilla was a beautiful, blue-eyed blonde. She had undergone a dramatic conversion and had come to work in the Sailors' Home in Shanghai. Charley had gone there to witness among the English-speaking sailors, since he could not manage the local dialect. He was soon attracted by Priscilla and it was not long before she had agreed to marry him. She was taking on a very temperamental and individualistic person, but she always loved him deeply, though she found him increasingly hard to understand. They were married first by Pastor Hsi and then again, officially, by the Consul. This gentleman was rather shocked by the casual appearance of the bridal couple; Charley wearing his usual rough calico Chinese gown and Priscilla having merely added to her gown a long white sash, bearing the words 'United to fight for Jesus'. It was an unconventional start to an unconventional marriage. They set off to work and make a home in Lungan, South Shanxi. Charley was now discovered to be an asthma sufferer. Mountainous areas caused him much discomfort and a struggle for breath, so also did the old-fashioned Chinese-style clay boilers, which belched fumes through a hole in the roof.

Lungan was not an easy place to work as it contained 10,000 Muslims and many spirit worshippers. As soon as they reached their house, people broke in and ran all over it like ants, and were abusive and unpleasant. For five whole years, the Studds never left home without rudeness being hurled at them, and they were held responsible for a period of drought.

There was much to upset Priscilla, such as public executions, which she forced herself to watch for the sake of the poor creatures dragged to the scaffold.

Missionary wives saw many strange things. It might be the wedding of a *ku-niang*, a young girl of over twelve. She would be kept at home until a marriage was arranged for her. When this time came, on the day before the wedding, all her belongings would be taken to the home of her future husband. Clothing, crockery, bedding, all were displayed publicly on tables covered with red cloth, and carried in procession through the street, headed by a band of musicians. The following day, about five in the morning, awakened by music, the bride would be taken to her new home and husband in a grand red satin sedan chair. The missionary wives knew that such elaborate ceremonies did not always mean happiness for the young bride, sometimes yoked to men they did not care for and under the future domination of the mother-in-law.

And Priscilla, like all the missionary ladies, was always deeply sad at the sight of little girls suffering with their newly-bound feet, as was still the custom in those days for girls of wealthier families.

Charley and Priscilla soldiered on and tried all ways of drawing followers. They were both radical Christians and were much attracted by Salvation Army methods of bold declamation and public witness. Thus they held processions, with drums and with Charley playing the banjo, at which he excelled. It was all very noisy and showy. Hudson was not pleased when he heard about this. He knew that such displays often antagonised the Chinese scholars who were so influential, and that too much of this kind of thing could end with them all being bundled out of the mission station.

Charley and Priscilla enjoyed a blissful married life and soon Priscilla was expecting their first baby. They decided to have the baby at Lungan although there was no resident doctor or nurse. At the birth, Priscilla was very ill and the nurse who came from a distance was of the opinion that Mrs Studd should 'go home to England'. This annoyed Charley who said, 'God never sent us here to make us fools.' He felt he was acting scripturally when he anointed his wife with oil and prayed over her. She certainly recovered and grew stronger, though her heart was always weak. In the years that followed, Priscilla had four daughters, but like her colleague Mary Louisa Cassels, she too lost a baby boy. Childbirth was hazardous in the climate and the circumstances of the mission stations.

Poor Priscilla was very upset at losing her baby boy. 'I felt absolutely heartbroken', she said. 'But I made a mark in my Bible. I made a covenant with God. I was not going to let sorrow of any kind come into my life and ruin my life as a missionary.' Yet she also lost another baby son in England later.

In 1889, Charley and Priscilla purchased a good property for the work in Lungan and were joined by their friends Stanley Smith and his wife. As well as a church, they established an opium refuge, though it was not easy to work with the fiery Pastor Hsi. In seven years nearly 1,000 men and women passed through the refuge. They also ran a dispensary, with the aid of a couple of simple medical books and a few homely remedies. They found their life very exciting, and they refused to be daunted by difficulties. 'Impossibilities have no real place in the real Christian's vocabulary,' said Charley. 'Some of us have only the jawbone of an ass – but what a mighty weapon that is when surrendered to the Lord!'

Chapter 9

Times of Trial

In 1900, the flashes of trouble that had erupted all over China for years ignited and flared up into a terrible flame. The rumblings of discontent and the effects of heavy taxation caused riots and rebellion. China became involved in a war with Japan and lost Korea to Japan and Port Arthur to Russia. The Chinese realised that their country must adapt to Western ways to increase their fighting power. Internal reforms too were needed. The young Emperor Guangxu drew together some radical thinkers and they produced the 'One Hundred Days Reform'.

But they had reckoned without the old Dowager Empress Ci Xi, a power behind the throne from the 1860s onward. She was totally set in her ways and absolutely resisted any changes and at once cancelled those that had been made. She seized the reins of government, imprisoned the Emperor, executed many of the court and government officials. And once more 'foreign devils' were blamed and had to be got rid of.

She issued a terrible proclamation to be pasted on all walls in China. It said that 'All foreigners should be killed.' Since most foreigners were missionaries, this was a dreadful thing for the China Inland Mission and their colleagues to learn.

Gangs of young Chinese men, members of secret societies, rampaged round the country attacking and murdering anyone not obviously Chinese. These young men were called 'Boxers' because of the public displays of Chinese boxing they used to recruit members. Some of these fanatics actually believed they could render themselves magically immune to bullets. The Empress supported these thugs.

The Foreign Legations in Peking – buildings housing representatives of foreign governments – were in a state of siege. People on their staff could not easily move in or out and food became scarce. Outside, the bands of fearful Boxers were waiting. It was a time of terror.

Hudson Taylor was touring in Australia at this time, speaking about the work of the mission. When telegrams reached him reporting loss of people and property and the threat to Chinese Christians, he was fearfully upset and grew very depressed.

At last a force of united foreign troops landed in China and fought their way to Peking, entered the city and, after much bloodshed, raised the siege of the Legations. The poor frightened people within the Legations could now get out and obtain food, and let their families and friends know that they were still alive. But the forces of the Chinese Empire felt that they had been humiliated on their own soil. The court fled from the capital.

The fortifications built by the Chinese were now knocked down and apologies and large sums of money in reparation were demanded from China by the foreign governments.

Gradually, the Boxer terror subsided and some sort of normality returned. The full fury of the troubles had fallen on the north and east of China, and Szechwan was less seriously affected since the Viceroy had decided to ignore many orders from Peking. But the Consul at Chunking had advised Willie Cassels, in the summer of 1900, to leave Paoning and go to safety since news had come of some missionaries being killed. Willie did not want to leave and did not hurry off – he felt he was needed and his colleagues too. In letters to them, he encouraged them rather than urged them to leave. In August, however, all the missionary ladies were sent to the coast for more secure accommodation in Shanghai and finally Willie himself was persuaded to leave and spent three months in Shanghai, wondering all the time about his people. In 1895, Willie had been consecrated the first Bishop of the Anglican Church in western China and his great pastoral gifts fully recognised. But in Szechwan during the rising, he had been a liability.

A year later it seemed safe for him to return. On an exhausting journey up the Yangtze gorges, he was nearly shipwrecked, but, on arrival in Paoning, he realised that the tide of hostility had ebbed and there was again a chance for the expansion of the Gospel.

* * * * * *

Stanley Smith and his wife were still working in Eastern Shanxi but had decided to break their official links with the China Inland Mission. Stanley felt that he differed rather strongly from Hudson Taylor on some points of theology and would feel happier if he worked independently. There was no break in their good personal relations and Stanley and Hudson Taylor remained on excellent terms of friendship.

The second of the seven who severed official links with the mission was, not surprisingly, Charley Studd. He continued to be very independent. But he too remained on terms of close friendship with Hudson Taylor and the other members of the mission. He did find though that some of his radical practices, like the use of drums and banjos and processions to advertise the Gospel, did not go down well in China. But you could not tell Charley much – he had to find things out for himself.

Priscilla, his wife, continued to support Charley and showed great personal skills in evangelising. Sometimes, rather dangerously, she would go off in a springless cart to preach in neighbouring areas. She was unafraid. In spite of the personal questions thrown at her, the staring and poking, she retained her dignity and took every opportunity to tell the Gospel story. 'I've come to bring you good news', she would say with a smile. Charley said of her, 'She speaks not from books, nor from the study, nor even from meditation; she speaks from vision and from communion.' He was very proud of her.

Neither of them knew good health. Charley's asthma grew so uncontrollable that it finally came to him that he would have to return to England to restore his health. Hudson came to see them before they left China. Generously, as was his habit, Charley told Hudson that he was making a gift to the CIM of the Studd premises for the development of their work. Hudson would have preferred to look after the premises for Charley to return to but Studd was determined. 'So I accepted it', said Hudson, 'and when I got to Lungan I was much pleased with the work.'

So Charley, Priscilla and their four daughters left China. They had worked there for nearly ten years since Charley came out as one of the original Cambridge Seven. In Shanghai, in front of the ship's company, their Chinese Christian friends were sobbing. As Charley waved goodbye one of the passengers said: 'Well, Mr Studd, you did not come out to China for nothing.'

This was true. Ever since his arrival, Charley had worked flat out, and his personal life had been one of self-denial and sacrifice. He had lived an ascetic life, giving up comfort, eating anything and expecting much the same standards from his wife and daughters, and also from his colleagues and his converts. And he had worked wonders in the opium clinics.

* * * * * *

Mercifully, the other members of the seven had escaped the worst rigours of the Boxer Rebellion but had gone through many dangerous and uncomfortable moments. Cecil Polhill, with a fine Chinese companion, had begun a new work in the Tibetan area of Sungpan. Lo Wang could read and write, do rough work and care for the horse and baggage. At Sungpan, Wang was left in charge and during Cecil's brief absence local threats turned into violence. When Cecil returned, the drought was attributed to the foreign god, and the family and Wang were bound and hustled before the magistrate. Wang begged to be punished to appease the mob. He was beaten till his legs were raw, and a heavy wooden collar was put round his neck. Finally, the crowd dispersed. Wang had been punished for being a Christian, but afterwards he kept saying, 'It was nothing; it was for Jesus's sake.' Soon Lo Wang was baptised.

Before the Boxer uprising, Cecil Polhill and his wife became involved in one of the 'flash riots' that had blown up for years. They almost lost their lives but were miraculously delivered. They found themselves much attached to the remote Tibetan people and spent all their working lives round the borders of Tibet. Like many Europeans, Cecil found his health affected by the climate and was several times sent back to England for recuperation, but he always returned. His heart was in China and he made seven return visits. 'The Lord make us to be inextinguishable firebrands' was his constant prayer.

Dick Hoste continued to work with Pastor Hsi until the pastor died in Shanxi in 1896. In 1901, Dick was appointed Acting General Director of the China Inland Mission and in 1903, when Hudson Taylor died, Dick became head of the mission. He remained in Shanghai and managed the mission for over thirty years. He was a man of exceptional goodness, yet he was not severe, but attracted everyone. Wise and gentle, he possessed the right qualities for his job, as Hudson had foreseen many years earlier. He was indeed the man to follow Hudson.

Chapter 10

Ongoing Mission

To the ends of their lives the Cambridge Seven witnessed for Christ and glorified God. They never looked back and despite the trials and tribulations which came to some of them, they all considered it a privilege to have been allowed to 'go out' for Christ.

At various conferences they would get together and great would be the talking and laughing and exchanging of memories and incidents and family news. All seven married and a high proportion of their large families followed in their footsteps and became missionaries also. Just as Hudson Taylor had known the thrill of having sons alongside him in the mission's work, so did several of the seven know the joy of travelling with their own children when grown-up, to some outpost.

Although the terrors and errors of the Boxer rising were over, there was no real stability. In the first decade of the new century the Manchu dynasty was moving to a collapse. This took place in 1911. Revolutionaries set up a provisional government in Nanjing, and Sun Yat Sen was the first provisional president in 1912. There were regional rivalries for the next few years and the real power lay in the hands of the regional warlords. Through all these upheavals, the proclamation of Christ went on.

* * * * * *

Bishop Willie Cassels was forever travelling and in the year 1910 he visited all stations in his diocese, several more than once. To journey across the diocese in western China from east to west involved a month of continuous movement. The Bishop's eldest daughter, Jessie, called her father, 'My idea of a man – physically strong and courageous and sportsmanlike . . . interested in so many things.' Later, she recalled days spent on the road in China with him. 'How thoughtful he was, not only for me, but for our servant and the coolies – it was the same. Inquisitive crowds did not bother him, nor rumours of bandits, danger of flood, danger by fire, danger of precipices, danger of sickness and accident – these were all met in the same undaunted way and because he was in the path of his work, he always came unflinchingly through.' So wrote Jessie.

The Bishop and his wife both fell ill in 1925, probably from typhus, and despite prayers, nothing could be done for them and before long William passed away. His wife died shortly afterwards. Family letters reveal that people crowded from all parts of the diocese, both foreign and Chinese. 'The funeral was remarkable in that the whole city turned out. The head magistrate and his wife both came and brought flowers.'

Their daughter said, 'Father was so proud of Mother's courage and that she had been used to bring so many women to Jesus. He felt that if she had not been so brave he could not have left her for his long journeys.' And of her father, Jessie said: 'He was always a hero to me, strong and silent and wholehearted in his work.'

* * * * * *

Stanley Smith's son, Geoffrey, although he did not work in China, became a medical missionary in East Africa, and was plainly made of the same stuff as his father.

Monty Beauchamp had continued his hard evangelistic journeys, always carrying a large palm-leaf fan attached to a stick, with big letters on it – 'Repent, the Kingdom of Heaven is at hand.'

'Won't you come and help to run the estate?' pleaded his eldest brother, who had no sons of his own. He offered Monty a substantial fortune if he would do this, but Monty had said 'no'. He loved China. In the Rising of 1900, he had reluctantly allowed himself to be sent home for a couple of years but was back again in China in 1902. He 'retired' as he thought, but during the first Great War in Europe he was ordained as a chaplain to the forces. One brother and his own eldest son were killed. Later, Monty inherited the family title. Strong and active still he toured again in the land he loved. But sickness overtook him and, nearly eighty, he died at his son's mission station in Paoning in 1939. He was far from the family mansion in Norfolk, but he was in the place where his heart had been for sixty years.

Arthur Polhill-Turner survived the troubles that followed the Boxer rising and did not retire until he was nearly seventy, when he took a country living in Hertfordshire and continued to speak the word of God. His brother Cecil died eventually at the family seat at Howbury, at almost eighty years old.

Dick Hoste, watching carefully over the fortunes of the CIM, remained in Shanghai and was interned by the Japanese in 1944. He left China the following year, weakened and aged by his experiences, and died in London, the last of the seven, in 1946. Under his leadership, despite civil war and revolution, the strength in numbers of the mission staff increased from 716 when he took over to 1,326 when he retired.

The most important quality for someone superintending a mission, Dick had said, 'was a capacity to appreciate the gifts and powers of widely different kinds of workers and then to help them along the lines of their own personalities.' Dick was a humble and much-loved leader.

* * * * * *

After leaving China, a whole new saga opened for the Studds. They never returned to China, but their missionary zeal did not abate. Since Charley had earlier given away all his money, the provision for his wife and four daughters was a delicate matter in which he was much helped by his mother and family. But he could not regret what he had seen as a direct command from his Lord. He spent six years working in India, probably thinking to show some appreciation for the fortune his father had accumulated there through his business interests and which had given Charley and his brothers and sisters such a privileged childhood.

When over fifty years old, Charley set off for Africa. Here he formed the Heart of Africa Mission and the Worldwide Evangelisation Crusade and, through his flamboyant personality, affected many lives. He did not feel it was right for his wife to go with him to Africa; she had poor health and Charley preferred that she remain at home and sustain him by her prayers and active propagation of the missionary cause. This was very hard for Priscilla. Apart from a fourteen-day visit to Africa, prior to her death, she did not see her husband for years at a time.

Yet whatever one might have thought of the 'Banjo Bwana' as he was known, his eccentric behaviour and amazing self-confidence, one could not but admire him. Old, sick and tired, he pressed on to the end. His son-in-law, Alfred Buxton, said, 'C.T.'s life stands as some rugged Gibraltar – an eternal rebuke to easy-going Christianity.' Charley died in the Belgian Congo in 1931, and a thousand Africans followed him to his grave.

When the Cambridge Seven set off from Victoria Railway Station in 1885, they had no idea of what lay before them. But they put their trust in God and all believed the words uttered then by Stanley Smith: 'Surely God is strong enough to fight our battles and surely God is rich enough to supply our needs. And surely God is wise enough to teach us and direct our paths.'

And so it proved.